Animals Hide

Patricia Brennan

Rigby

Here is a grasshopper.
Can you see it?

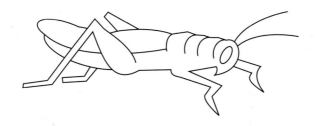

3

Here is a bird.
Can you see it?

Here is a frog.
Can you see it?

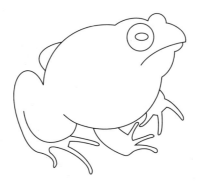

Here is a mouse.

Can you see it?

Here is a rabbit.

Can you see it?

Here is a lizard.
Can you see it?

Here is a snake.

Can you see it?

Here is a lion.

Can you see it?